DESIGN and MAKE

Water Projects

John Williams

WAYLAND

DESIGN and MAKE

Houses and Homes
Simple Machines
Things to Wear
Toys and Games
Wheels and Transport

First published in 1997 by Wayland Publishers Ltd,
61 Western Road, Hove, East Sussex BN3 1JD, England
© Copyright 1997 Wayland Publishers Ltd
Series planned and produced by Margot Richardson
Find Wayland on the internet at http://www.wayland.co.uk

British Library Cataloguing in Publication Data
Williams, John, 1936–
Water Projects. – (Design & Make)
1.Water – Juvenile literature
2.Hydraulic engineering – Juvenile literature
3.Handicraft – Juvenile literature
I.Title
745.5

ISBN 0 7502 2100 3

Commissioned photography by Zul Mukhida
Cover photography by APM Studios
Designed by Tim Mayer
Edited by Margot Richardson
Equipment supplied by Technology Teaching Systems Ltd, Alfreton, UK
Printed and bound in Italy by G. Canale & C.S.p.A., Turin

CONTENTS

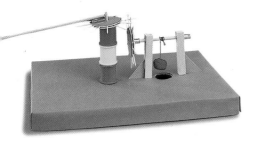

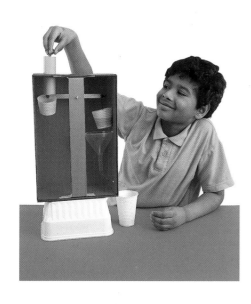

INTRODUCTION

Two-thirds of the earth's surface is covered by water. On it, ships carry cargo made in factories, dug out of the earth or grown for food. Although people travel long distances in trains and aeroplanes, even today many people driving cars or lorries have to make short journeys on ferry boats.

Boats and water are also used for enjoying ourselves. Visit the seaside and you will see people on surf-boards, water-skis, yachts, or just swimming.

Water is very important for growing food. In some places where there is not enough rain, people have designed clever machines for getting water out of rivers or wells and on to the land.

Big ships sail all over the world carrying cargo. To make loading the cargo easier, it is often put into large steel boxes, called containers.

Some people live on boats, rather than on dry land. These are houseboats in Bangladesh.

For thousands of years, water has been an important source of power. Before motors were invented water was used to drive mill wheels joined to all sorts of machines. These machines were often for grinding wheat, but there were also machines for crushing rocks and minerals. It has only been within the last 250 years that other forms of energy – such as electricity – have become available.

This book will help you to design and make some of these machines and boats, and to learn how to use water to help us in many ways.

This water slide uses the force of running water so that people can enjoy themselves.

INFLATABLE BOAT

Some small boats are made from rubber or plastic filled with air. This makes them easy to keep when they are not being used because the air can be let out and the boat can be folded up. This model is made from a balloon and some plastic. If the balloon is hard to blow up, ask an adult to help you.

YOU WILL NEED

- Long modelling balloon
- Plastic bubble-wrap
- Plastic parcel tape
- Corrugated plastic
- Plain paper
- Felt-tip pen
- Pencil
- Scissors
- Balloon pump

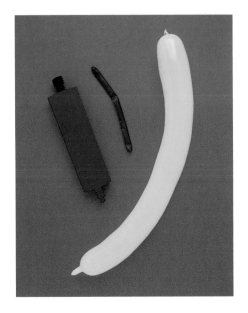

1 Ask an adult to help you to blow up the balloon, using the balloon pump. Let some air out and tie a knot in the end.

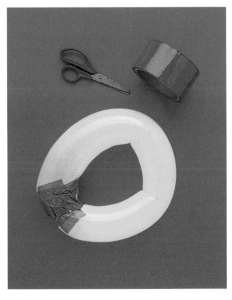

2 Bend the balloon into a circle and stick the ends together firmly with parcel tape.

Inflatable boats can be made in many different shapes. Some are used to rescue people who get into trouble at sea. Others are just for having fun, such as on holiday.

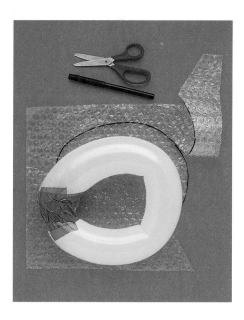

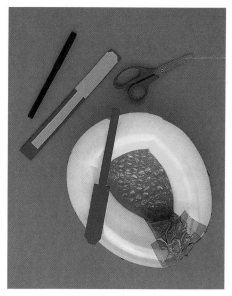

3 Put the balloon circle on the smooth side of the plastic bubble-wrap. Draw round the outside with a felt-tip pen. Cut out the shape.

4 Using small pieces of parcel tape, stick the base of the boat to the sides. Make sure there are no gaps, so the boat will be quite waterproof.

5 Design some oars to go with the boat. Draw their shape on plain paper and cut it out. Use the shape as a template and cut two oars from the corrugated plastic.

NOW TRY THIS

Inflatable boats are often used for life rafts, if a bigger boat sinks. People in a life raft, waiting to be rescued, would need to shelter from the weather. Design and make a cover to go over the boat. To keep out the rain, what should it be made from?

SHADUF

Shadufs have been used to get water out of rivers for thousands of years. Instead of lifting the water up by hand, a shaduf uses a lever and a heavy weight to do the work.

People made shadufs from whatever they could find around them, such as logs of wood tied together with rope, and stones. Here is a model to make that uses the same type of natural materials.

Shadufs were mostly used many years ago, before better machines were invented, but they are sometimes still seen in Middle Eastern countries, such as Egypt.

YOU WILL NEED

- Forked stick, approx 15cm long
- Straight stick, approx 25cm long
- Modelling clay (eg Plasticine)
- Small stones
- Netting vegetable bag
- Thin card or foil
- String
- Scissors

1 Make the modelling clay into a ball. Push the forked stick into it so that it stands upright.

2 Cut a piece from the vegetable netting. Put the stones on it and tie them into a small bag.

3 Make a small bucket from card or foil. Make a handle from string and tie it on.

4 Cut two pieces of string about 20cm long. Take the long straight stick. Tie the bag of stones on one end and the bucket on the other.

5 Put the long stick in the fork of the other stick so that it balances. Tie it on loosely with another piece of string.

6 Try lifting some water with the bucket. When the lever is balanced, water can be lifted without much effort.

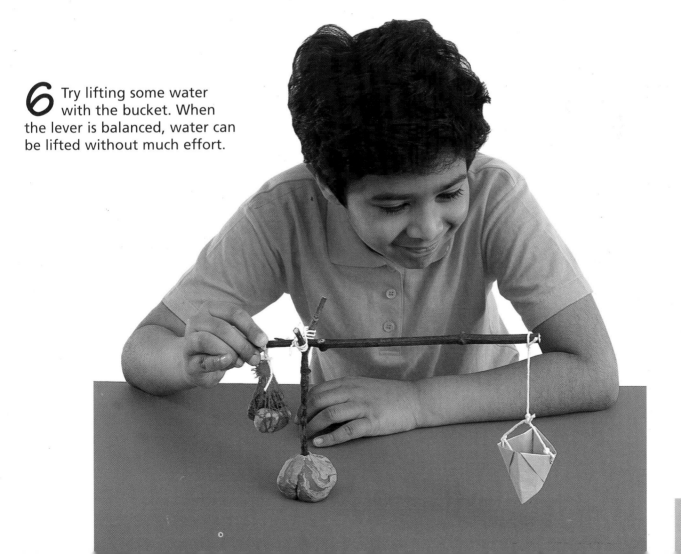

WATER CLOCK

YOU WILL NEED

- Plastic bottle
- Stiff plastic or card
- Wooden dowel, approx 5mm diameter, a little longer than bottle
- Cotton reel
- 1 x 1cm wood, about twice the length of bottle
- Rubber bands
- Masking tape
- PVA glue
- Pen or pencil
- Scissors
- Ruler
- Hole punch
- Junior hacksaw
- Waterproof container
- Plastic tube and tap (optional)

People first found a way of measuring time in about 1500 BC. They made sundials which used shadows made by the sun. However, sundials could not work at night or on cloudy days, so another way of telling the time was needed. Water clocks were used until clocks with pendulums were invented, in about the 1600s.

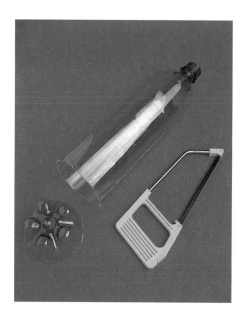

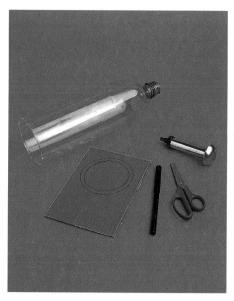

1 Ask an adult to help you cut off the bottom of the bottle, using the hacksaw.

2 Stand the bottle on the card or plastic and draw round it. Draw a slightly smaller circle inside this and cut it out. Make a 4mm hole in the centre.

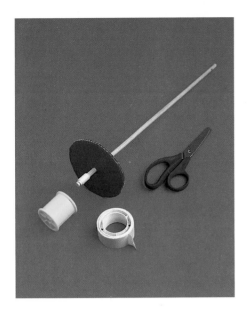

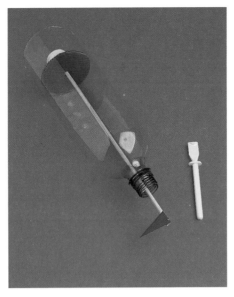

3 Push the circle on to the dowel. It should fit tightly. Wind some masking tape around the end of the dowel. Push the cotton reel on over the masking tape and make sure it fits tightly.

4 Push the other end of the dowel through the top of the bottle. Make a small pointer from card and glue it on the top. Let the glue dry.

5 Join the piece of square-section wood to the bottle with two or three rubber bands. Stand the water clock in a waterproof container.

6 Let water run or drip down and watch the pointer rise up. Measure how fast it moves against a clock, and mark intervals on the length of wood.

NOW TRY THIS

Make another type of water clock that is like an alarm clock. It uses a balloon and a pin. Put the blown-up balloon at the top of the tall 1 x 1cm wood. Put the pin pointing upwards on the dowel. When the dowel gets to the top, the pin bursts the balloon.

WATER WHEEL

Falling water has energy that can make objects move. Before electricity was discovered, water was used to drive machines. Today, we use the power of water to drive generators and make electricity.

YOU WILL NEED

- Two thick card circles, approx 6cm diameter, with 4mm centre holes
- Eight pieces wooden dowel, approx 5mm diameter and 5cm long
- Four pieces corrugated plastic, each 5 x 5cm
- Waxed drink carton
- One piece wooden dowel, approx 5mm diameter and 7.5cm longer than width of carton
- Two pieces PVC tube, approx 5mm diameter and 1cm long, slit down side
- Thread
- Modelling clay (eg Plasticine)
- PVA glue
- Hole punch
- Pencil
- Ruler
- Scissors
- Pencil sharpener

The Laxey Wheel was built in 1854 on the Isle of Man, part of the UK. It was designed to pump water out of nearby mines. It has a diameter of 22 metres, and is the biggest water wheel in the world.

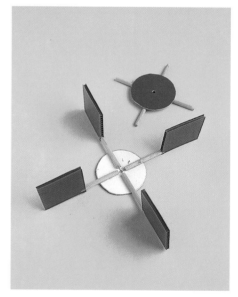

1 Divide the card circles into four equal parts, drawing lines with a pencil and ruler. Glue a piece of dowel along each line, so they stick out the same distance at each end. Let the glue dry.

2 Take one of the card and dowel circles. Push a piece of plastic on the end of each dowel. It may help to sharpen the dowels a little first with a pencil sharpener.

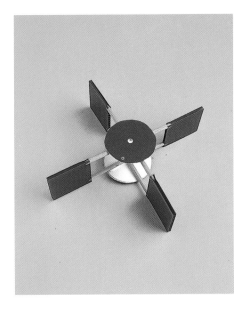

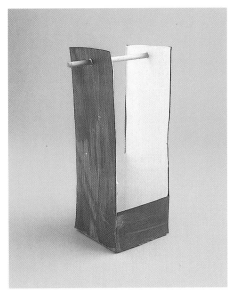

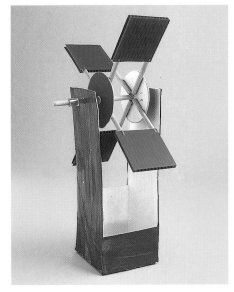

3 Take the other circle and do the same, so the the two circles are joined up.

4 Cut off the top and two opposite sides of the carton. Make two holes in the other sides, opposite each other. They must be big enough so the dowel can turn freely.

5 Push the long dowel through a hole in the carton, then through the water wheel, and out the other side. Make it longer on one side than the other. Fix it in place with the pieces of PVC tube.

6 Tie a piece of thread to the long end of the dowel axle and fix a weight (such as a lump of modelling clay) to the other end. Put the water wheel under a stream of water.

NOW TRY THIS

Fix a cotton reel on the axle of the water wheel. Make sure it fits tightly. Stick the end of the thread to the cotton reel. What happens to the weight? Does it move faster or slower?

FLAT-BOTTOM FERRY

YOU WILL NEED

- Waxed drink carton
- Stiff cardboard
- Four paper clips
- Two metal paper fasteners
- 8cm wooden dowel, approx 5mm diameter
- Cotton reel
- Two small pieces PVC tube, approx 5mm diameter, slit down side
- Parcel tape
- Thick thread
- Scissors
- Ruler
- Hole punch

People often need to cross rivers, but they do not always have bridges over them. Ferries with flat bottoms can cross rivers, carrying cars, animals and people. This sort of ferry is usually joined to a metal cable. An engine on the ferry winds the cable around a pulley which pulls the ferry across the river.

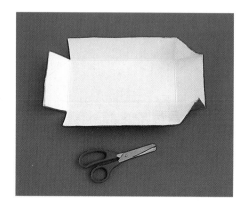

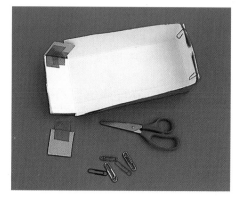

1 Cut the carton in half lengthways. One end should open out and fold up neatly. Make a cut down the other two corners and fold the narrow ends out flat.

2 Cut two squares of card. Each side should be the same size as the carton sides. Stick them on to the flat ends with parcel tape and fold them on the join. Fold the ends up again and hold them in place with paper clips.

Flat ferries have a ramp at each end so that people can get on at one side of the river, and walk or drive off at the other. This ferry is in China.

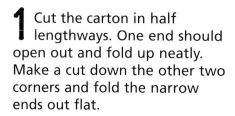

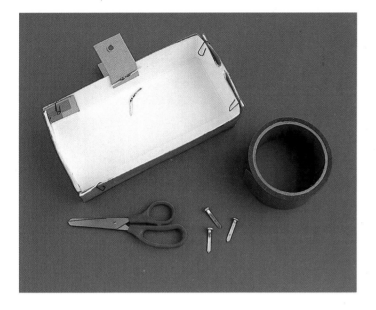

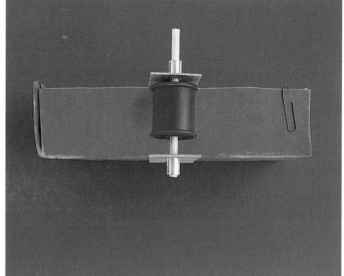

3 Cut two rectangles of stiff card, about 6 x 3cm. Make a 5mm hole in each one, about 1.5cm from the end. Fold one piece in half. Join the folded one to the side and the straight one to the bottom, using paper fasteners.

4 Wind some masking tape around the middle of the dowel. Push a cotton reel over the masking tape, so it fits tightly. Push the ends of the dowel through the two holes in the card. Put a piece of PVC tube on each end to hold the dowel in place.

5 Join the thread to the edge of a water container, wind it around the cotton reel once and join it to the opposite side. It should not be too tight. Wind the dowel with your fingers and the ferry will go across the water. Either end of the ferry can go down to let cars on and off.

NOW TRY THIS

Make a handle for the winch that winds the cable around the pulley. Cut a circle of card about 5cm diameter. Punch a 4mm hole in the centre, and another hole near the edge. Glue a small piece of dowel in the hole near the edge. Glue the centre hole on the top of the dowel that goes through the cotton reel.

TORPEDO FISH

YOU WILL NEED

- Small plastic drink bottle with screw-on lid (approx 23cm high)
- Plastic propeller, approx 15cm long
- Piece of corrugated plastic or balsa wood, approx 30 x 10cm.
- Several thick rubber bands
- Medium paper clip
- Small plastic bead
- Small piece of dowel
- Bradawl

Take care when using a bradawl to make holes.

- **Hold the object in a vice if possible.**
- **Ask an adult to show you what to do.**

This project works a little like a torpedo, and also like a fish. The energy stored in a wound-up rubber band drives the fish along, and the fin keeps the body even in the water.

1 Use the bradawl to make a hole in the middle of the bottom of the plastic bottle. Also make a hole in the bottle top.

2 Unbend the paper clip, leaving a hook in one end. Push the other end through the bottle top, bead and propeller. Bend the end of the paper clip tightly over the centre of the propeller.

Fish have fins on the top and bottom of their body, at the sides, and on their tails. They use their fins to move themselves along and to steer.

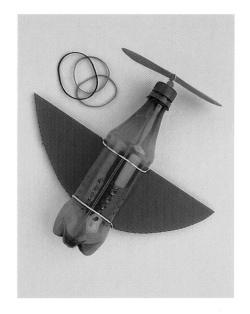

3 Tie a piece of string to the rubber band. Push the string through the hole in the bottom of the bottle. Put the dowel through the rubber band and pull the rest of the band through into the bottle.

4 Hook the rubber band on to the paper clip in the bottle top. Cut the string off and screw the top back on the bottle.

5 Cut a fin from a piece of balsa wood or corrugated plastic. It should have one curved side, about 10cm at its widest point. Join it to the bottle with rubber bands.

6 Undo the top a little and let the bottle half fill with water. Tighten the lid again. Wind up the propeller as far as possible, and let it go in the water.

CATAMARAN

Most boats have one hull that floats on the water. A catamaran has two hulls, which make it wider and harder to tip over when it is sailing.

When you need to use a hand drill to make a hole, ask an adult to help you and to show you what to do.

YOU WILL NEED

- Small plastic drink bottle (approx 23cm high)
- Piece of balsa wood, approx 5mm thick and 28 x 5cm
- Three pieces of dowel, approx 5mm diameter and same length as plastic bottle
- Piece of dowel, approx 5mm diameter and 35cm long
- Cotton reel
- 12 rubber bands
- Thread
- Tissue paper, fabric or plastic (for sail)
- PVA glue
- Masking tape
- Junior hacksaw
- Drill with 5mm drill bit

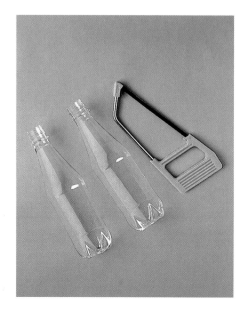

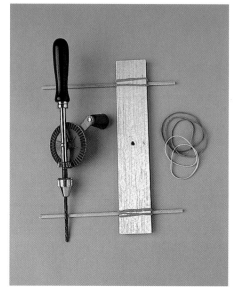

1 Ask an adult to help you cut the plastic bottle in half lengthways, using the hacksaw. Hold the bottle in a vice if possible.

2 Drill a hole in the centre of the balsa wood. Using rubber bands, join two pieces of dowel to the balsa wood, on either side of the hole.

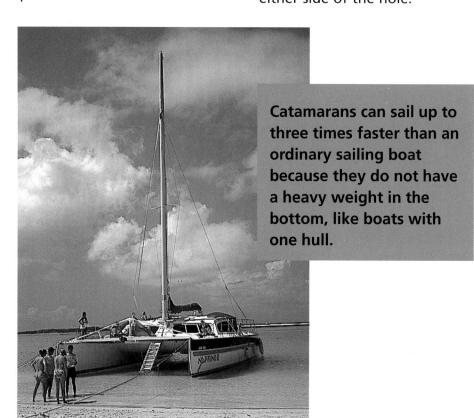

Catamarans can sail up to three times faster than an ordinary sailing boat because they do not have a heavy weight in the bottom, like boats with one hull.

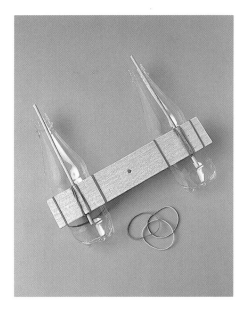

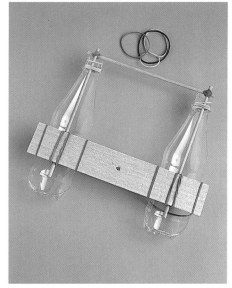

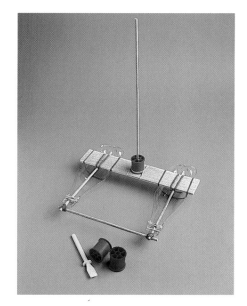

3 Put the balsa wood and dowels over the plastic bottle halves. Join the balsa to the bottles with more rubber bands. Make sure the bottles are the same distance from each end of the balsa wood.

4 Wind rubber bands round the neck ends of the bottles. Join the third piece of dowel to the others, at right angles. Use more rubber bands to hold them together.

5 Put the cotton reel over the hole in the balsa wood. Hold it in place with another rubber band. Put some glue on the end of the mast and push it down into the hole in the wood. Let the glue dry.

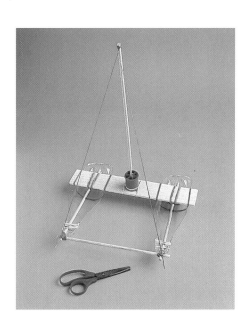

7 Make a sail from paper, plastic or fabric. It should be in the shape of a triangle. Stick the top of the sail to the mast with a little glue, and the bottom corners to the rigging with masking tape.

6 Add some rigging to make the mast stronger. Tie a thread to the front of the boat, then the top of the mast and down to the other side. Make sure it is tight.

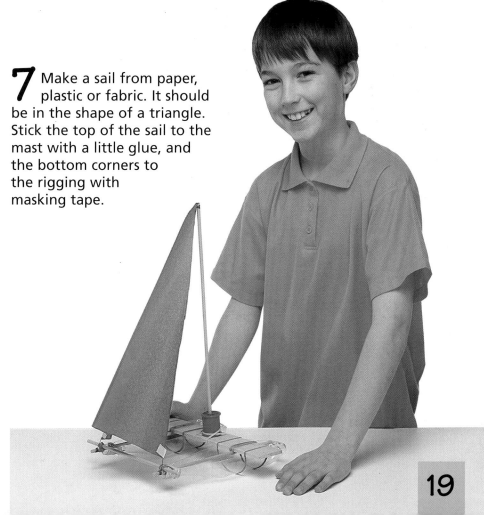

PADDLE BOAT

Take care when using a bradawl to make holes. See page 16.

Paddle boats were first built about 200 years ago. Sometimes they had a paddle wheel on either side, and others used one paddle at the back, like this model.

YOU WILL NEED

- Square-shaped plastic bottle, approx 25cm high
- Two pieces 1 x 1cm wood, about 1.5 times length of bottle
- Small piece of dowel, approx 2.5cm longer than width of bottle
- Cotton reel
- Recycled plastic food container lids
- Eight thin rubber bands
- One long thick rubber band
- Masking tape
- Scissors
- Plain paper
- Marker pen that will draw on plastic
- Ruler
- Stapler
- Bradawl

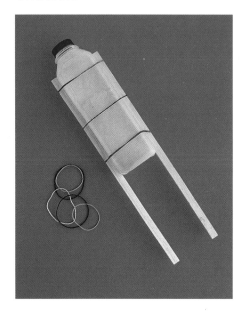

1 Put the pieces of 1 x 1cm wood on either side of the plastic bottle. Hold them together with several rubber bands.

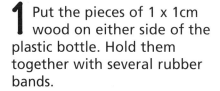

2 Draw the paddle shape on paper to make a template. It should look like a fat T shape. Make the top of the T the same width as the cotton reel. Use the paper template to mark out four shapes on the plastic lids. Cut the paddles out.

3 Stick the plastic paddles on to the cotton reel with masking tape. Make sure there is the same space between each one. Wind a rubber band round each side to hold them in place.

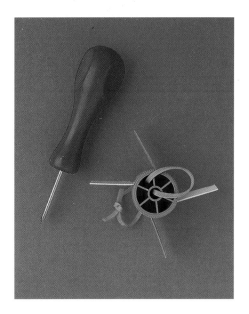

4 Ask an adult to help you use the bradawl to make a hole down one side of the cotton reel. Cut the thick rubber band and thread it through both holes. Tie it together again.

Paddle boats were mostly used on lakes and rivers in the 1800s. They did not work well on rough water, such as the sea.

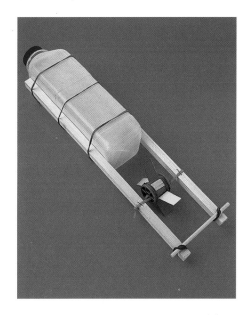

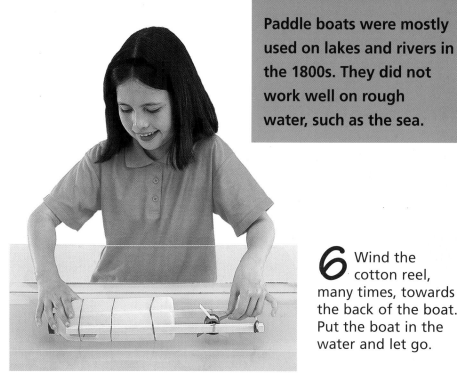

6 Wind the cotton reel, many times, towards the back of the boat. Put the boat in the water and let go.

5 Put the rubber band over the ends of the wood and slide it up towards the bottle. Staple the rubber band to the wood at the sides. Put the dowel across the ends of the wood. Join them together tightly with rubber bands.

NOW TRY THIS

Make a motor-driven paddle boat. Fix the cotton reel on a dowel axle. Mount a small electric motor (1.5V–4.5V) and 4.5V battery on top of the bottle. Join the spindle of the motor to the cotton reel with a rubber band.

SAKIA

This sakia in Egypt is being turned by a cow, which walks round and round in a circle all day. The sakia turns the wheel with the pots on it. The pots scoop up the water and pour it into a stream that runs on to the fields.

YOU WILL NEED

- Lid of a box, such as a shoe box

- Two pieces of 1 x 1cm wood, approx 8cm long

- Two or three cotton reels

- Three pieces wooden dowel, approx 5mm diameter: one 10cm, one 12cm, one 18cm long

- Four card circles approx 4cm diameter with 4mm centre holes

- Cocktail sticks or matchsticks

- Small pieces of PVC tube, approx 5mm diameter, slit down side

- Thread

- PVA glue

- Scissors

- Pencil

- Ruler

- Drill with 6mm drill bit

This is a simple machine that uses two special wheels called cogs to get water up out of a deep well. The cogs are made from card circles and cocktail or match sticks. They must be put on very carefully so that the distance between each stick is exactly the same.

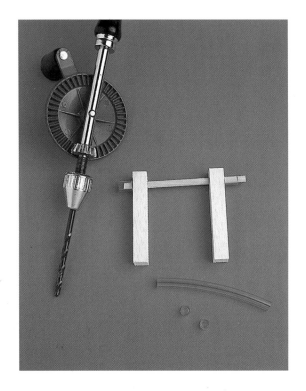

1 Ask an adult to help you drill a hole through each piece of 1 x 1cm wood, about 1cm from one end. Push the 10cm piece of dowel through and make sure it can turn freely. Put a piece of PVC tube on each end.

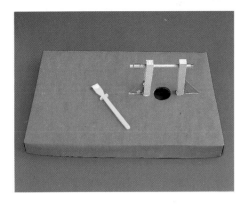

2 Cut a hole about 3cm diameter in the box lid. Glue the wood on either side of the hole. Glue small card triangles at the bottom to hold the wood more firmly. Let the glue dry.

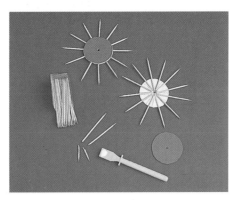

3 Divide each card circle into four, and then into twelve. Glue a stick on each line. When the glue is dry, glue a second card circle on top.

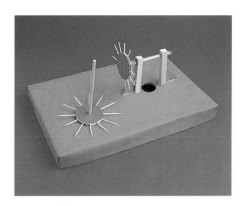

4 Put a cog on the end of the axle over the hole. You may have to break off the ends of the sticks so that the cog will fit. Put the other cog on the end of the 12cm dowel. Put some glue on the holes to stick the cogs on the dowels.

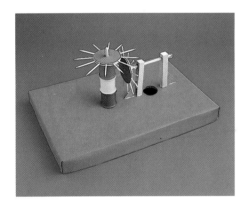

5 Glue three cotton reels together. Put them on the box, and put the dowel and cog down the centre hole. Work out where to put the cotton reels so that the cogs just meet. Then glue the bottom cotton reel to the box.

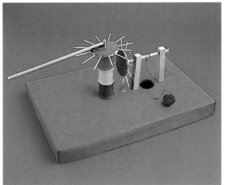

6 Glue the last piece of dowel to the top of the cog in the cotton reels. You may have to add some small pieces of card to make it high enough. Tie some thread to the axle over the hole. Put a weight, such as modelling clay, on the end of the thread.

7 When all the glue has dried, turn the long dowel. The axle over the hole will turn and bring up the 'bucket' out of the well.

DREDGER

- Two 30cm pieces of 1 x 1cm wood
- Six 6cm pieces of 1 x 1cm wood
- Four small card triangles
- Four pieces wooden dowel, approx 5mm diameter: two 15cm, one 18cm, one 3cm long
- Cotton reel
- Rubber bands
- Piece of recycled plastic bottle or tub
- Two plastic bottles
- Thick thread
- Small pieces of PVC tube about 5mm diameter, slit down side
- PVA glue
- Ruler
- Pencil
- Drill with 6mm drill bit

Sometimes rivers and harbours get clogged up with mud or sand. This stops boats going along because the water is not deep enough. To make the water deep again, a machine called a dredger is used to scoop up the soil or sand and put it somewhere else.

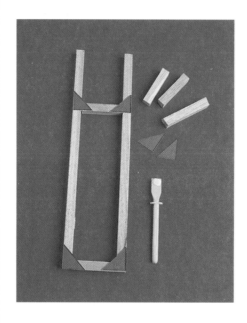

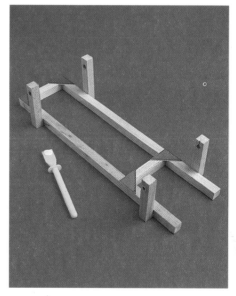

1 Take the two 30cm pieces of 1 x 1cm wood and two 6cm pieces and make the frame as shown in the photograph. Glue it together. Glue the card triangles over the joins to make them stronger.

2 Take the other four pieces of 1 x 1cm wood. In each piece drill a hole about 1cm from one end. (Ask an adult to help you with the drill.) Glue two pieces at each end of the long frame. The pieces should be about 5cm from the end and exactly opposite each other.

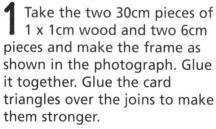

There are many different types of dredgers. Some suck up the mud through a big tube. Some use many buckets joined to a chain made into a circle, and others grab the mud, like the one in this photo.

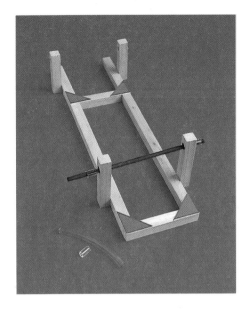

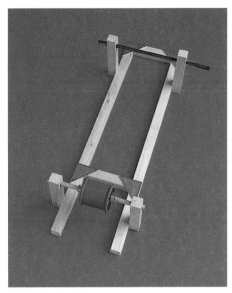

3 At the closed end of the frame, push a 15cm piece of dowel through the holes in the two uprights. Put pieces of PVC tube on each end to hold it in place.

4 Take the other 15cm dowel. Push it through a hole in the 1 x 1cm wood, the cotton reel and the other piece of wood. Put some glue on the holes in the wood. Add pieces of PVC tube on either side of the cotton reel to keep it in the centre.

5 Make the scoop. Take the 18cm piece of dowel. Cut a T-shaped piece of plastic. Fold up two sides of the plastic and join them to the dowel with rubber bands.

6 Join the scoop to the cotton reel with a rubber band so that it faces outwards. Cut a piece of thread about 30cm long. Tie one end to the scoop shaft and the other end to the dowel.

7 Join the dredger to the two plastic bottles with rubber bands. Float the dredger in some water. Tie it to the sides to stop it moving when it is being used. Wind the handle and the scoop will lift up.

FLOOD ALARM

During heavy rain, rivers and even dams may burst their banks and many houses and farms are flooded. People need a warning if this is going to happen so that they can move to higher ground. This project shows how to make an electric alarm that tells you when the water level is getting high.

YOU WILL NEED

- Plastic tube approx 4cm diameter
- Cork with diameter a little smaller than tube
- 1m single-core electrical wire
- Buzzer (or light bulb and bulb holder)
- Battery (4.5V minimum)
- Aluminium kitchen foil
- Masking or sticky tape
- Plastic tape
- Scissors
- Wire stripper and cutter
- Junior hacksaw
- Sink or tank same depth or deeper than the length of the tube

Because a big dam holds so much water, it could be very dangerous if it overflowed. An alarm would tell people when the water was getting near to the top of the wall.

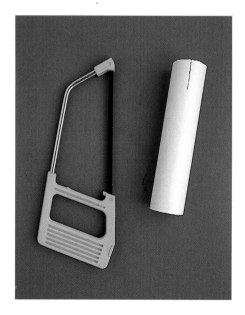

1 Ask an adult to help you use the hacksaw to cut a slit, about 3cm deep, at the top of the plastic tube. Use a vice to hold the tube while you are cutting it.

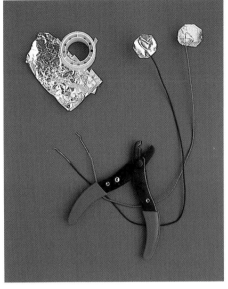

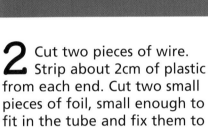

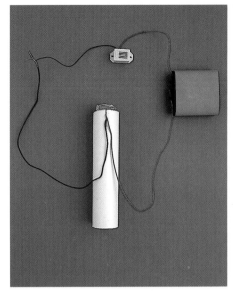

2 Cut two pieces of wire. Strip about 2cm of plastic from each end. Cut two small pieces of foil, small enough to fit in the tube and fix them to one end of the pieces of wire.

3 Slide the wires into the slit so that the two pieces of foil are at the top of the tube, one over the other. They should be close, but not touching.

4 Put the ends of the buzzer wires on the battery terminals to find out which way it works. Join one buzzer wire to the battery, and and the other to one of the loose wires. Join the other loose wire to the other battery terminal.

6 Slowly fill the sink or tank. As the water rises, the cork will float up the tube. When it reaches the top it will push the two pieces of foil together. When they touch, the buzzer will sound.

5 Tape the tube to the side of a sink or tank with plastic tape. Fill the tank so that the water just comes to the bottom of the tube. Put the cork in the bottom of the tube.

DRINK MACHINE

YOU WILL NEED

- Strong cardboard box, such as a shoe box, about 25 x 30 x 12cm
- Stiff card
- 15cm of 1 x 1cm wood
- Wooden dowel, approx 5mm diameter and 5cm longer than depth of box
- Two plastic cups, cut down to half their size
- Funnel (or cut-off end of plastic squeezy bottle)
- 15cm of PVC tube to fit end of funnel/bottle
- Narrow cardboard tube
- Drawing or mapping pins
- Thread
- Small weight (eg modelling clay)
- Metal paper fasteners
- PVA glue
- Masking or sticky tape
- Scissors
- Ruler
- Drill with 6mm drill bit

Here is an interesting machine that provides a drink when you drop a weight in the top of the box. A machine like this was first worked out by a famous Greek inventor called Hero, who lived more than 2,000 years ago.

Machines are used to sell many different things, from sweets and drinks to train tickets and maps. These machines are outside a shop in Japan.

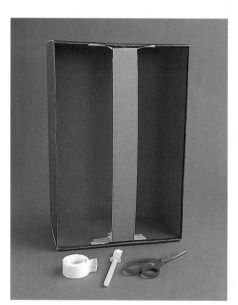

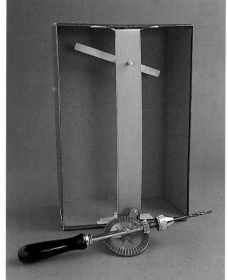

1 Cut a piece of stiff card about 5cm longer than the box and about 2.5cm wide. Fold over 2.5cm at either end. Glue it at either end so it runs down the centre of the box on the open side.

2 Ask an adult to help you drill a hole through the middle of the square-section wood. Make 5mm holes in the box and the card strip. They should be about 5cm from the top of the box and opposite each other. Push the dowel through a hole, the 1 x 1cm wood and out the other hole.

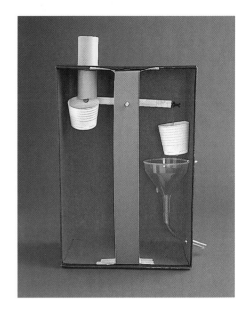

3 Pin a cup to one end of the wood. Cut a thread about 7.5cm long. Join a small piece of modelling clay to one end of it. Pin the top of thread to the other end of the wood.

4 Make a small hole in the bottom of the other cup. Join it to the side of the box with a paper fastener. Put a piece of PVC tube on the bottom of the funnel. Fix the funnel under the cup. Make a hole in the side of the box for the tube.

5 Make a hole in the top of the box for the cardboard tube. It should be over the left-hand cup.

NOW TRY THIS

● Can you think of a way of filling the cup again?

● Is there a continuous way of filling it up?

6 Make sure the plasticine weight is firmly covering the hole in the bottom of the cup. Fill it about half full with water. Put another cup under the end of the tube. Drop the marble down the cardboard tube at the top, and your drink will come out at the bottom.

GLOSSARY

alarm	Something that makes a sound at a set time, or when danger is near.
axle	A wood or metal rod on which a wheel turns.
balanced	Keeping a steady position, without falling over.
cable	A strong metal wire, used for electricity or to pull heavy loads.
cargo	Goods, not people, carried by ships, trains, aircraft or land transport.
cog	A wheel that has teeth sticking out from it, to turn another wheel.
diameter	The distance across the centre of a circle, from one side to the other.
dredging	Digging up mud or sand from under water.
energy	This is what enables all things, such as machines or animals, to do work.
fin	The parts of a fish that stick out from the main body. Machines can also have fins.
flood	When a lot of water covers land that is normally dry.
inflatable	Something that can be made bigger by pumping air into it, such as a tyre.
hull	The part of a boat or ship that floats in the water.
lever	A straight bar that does not bend, which can move something by pushing or pulling.
load	A weight that something has to carry, such as a person, truck or ship.
mast	A long pole on a boat or ship that holds up the sails.
paddle	Something that moves or is moved by water.
pulley	A special wheel around which a rope is pulled to raise a weight or move an object.
ramp	A straight slope that joins two different heights.
template	A shape used to mark and cut out a number of the same shapes.
terminal	The part of a battery where other things – such as wires – can be joined to it.
torpedo	An object, shaped like a bottle. It is fired from a submarine towards a ship, and it explodes when it hits the ship
triangle	A shape with three sides.
tube	A long hollow round shape, usually open at both ends.
volt (V)	A measurement of the 'push' or force, of electricity.
waterproof	Something that will not let water pass through it, such as plastic or glass.

BOOKS TO READ

Eyewitness Guides: Boat by Eric Kentley, Dorling Kindersley, 1992

Farmer Through History by Peter Chrisp, Wayland, 1992

Flood by Fred Martin, Heinemann Library, 1995

Natural Cycles: The Water Cycle by David Smith, Wayland, 1993

Our Green World: Oceans by John D Baines, Wayland, 1993

Technology in the Time of Ancient Egypt by Judith Crosher, Wayland, 1997

Understanding Geography: World Farming by Martin Bramwell, Usborne, 1994

The World's Rivers series, Wayland, 1992–93

The World's Transport: Water Travel by Eryl Davies, Wayland, 1992

TEACHERS' NOTES

Inflatable Boat With a little help, this simple boat is well within the capability of even the youngest children, although children under eight should be supervised while inflating the balloons. Such boats are used as life rafts in aeroplanes and ships, and children can be asked to invent special menus for survivors. The food should have high energy content, and should not need cooking.

Shaduf This simple device is based on the principle of the first-type lever, which has the load at one end, effort exerted at the other, and the fulcrum somewhere in between. Children should be encouraged to learn about levers when making this model. They could also be asked to design and make a more precise example of the mechanism, such as barriers used at car parks and road crossings.

Water Clock The ancient Egyptians were known to have used very accurate shadow clocks from about 1450BC, but it was much later that the Egyptian inventor, Ctesibius, built a workable water clock or *clepsydra*, on which this model is based. The problem with all water clocks is to keep the water in constant flow. Any deviation, and the time gaps vary. The parastatic or float clock helps to overcome this difficulty.

Water Wheel Until the advent of steam, the water wheel provided the main source of power for any kind of small industry. This is one of many designs that children can make. They should be encouraged to make the wheel do more than just rotate. They can experiment to see how much head of water is needed to lift varying weights. They can also see if it is better if the water makes contact with the wheel at the top, underneath, or halfway up the circumference. (About 200 years ago research found that halfway up was the best.)

Flat-Bottom Ferry The design of the hull for this boat allows for the roll-on, roll-off loading that most ferries use. This kind of chain link ferry has no direct motive power of its own, and is therefore used only for short distances. The only engine on the boat was used to wind in the chain, which pulled the boat across the river, and let it out the other end.

Torpedo Fish Most ships are driven through the water by a propeller, and the more of it that is under water the better. Children can experiment to see how deep they can make the fish lie in the water. The side fins stop the bottle rotating, and if flaps are fitted to these, they can act like a submarine's hydroplanes.

Catamaran This model can be developed further by the addition of a rudder, or by a change of sail rig. Most yachts use a fore-and-aft rig, and this can be made using a small length of dowel for the boom. Fix a clothes peg to the end of the dowel so that it can clip on to the mast. In this way the boom can swing from side to side depending on the direction of the wind. Like all sailing boats, the standing rigging is very important. No mast will stay up without it.

Paddle Boat This basic design works well over short distances. Children should be encouraged to find ways to increase the power of the paddle, and so give the boat a greater range, or be able to carry a heavier load. For many years there was much argument about which was the better, paddles or propellers/screws. It took a direct tug-of-war between two boats to settle the matter: the screw-driven boat won.

Sakia Unlike the Shaduf, which is used for lifting water over a short distance, the Sakia is a mechanism for using with a deep well. Care needs to be taken when making the cogs. The spokes must be evenly spaced and it helps if they are of equal length. It is possible to use a jig to make them in. Children should be encouraged to design a mechanism with different sized cogs, and to discover what effect this might have on the raising of the bucket, or on the speed that the animal has to walk.

Dredger This model is based on a design widely used in seventeenth-century Europe. The power was provided by one man, often working a treadmill. The dredger was floated on a pontoon made of two barges; for this model two plastic bottles have been used.

Flood Alarm Although this model suggests a way to avoid a possible catastrophe it could just as easily be used to stop a sink overflowing. Children will need to understand about basic electric circuits, so that they will realise the importance of closing the contacts. It is very important that they are made aware of the dangers of electricity, especially when associated with water. Only a small battery should be used.

Drink Machine This machine also includes a first-type lever. The weight is the plug in the water cup, and the effort is provided by the falling weight. The challenge in developing this machine is to design a method to refill the cup. The weight of water could be used to re-plug the cup, or perhaps a kind cistern could be designed similar to that used in Hero's original machine.

INDEX

Acknowledgements

The author and publishers wish to thank the following for their kind assistance with this book:
models Suhyun Haw, Yasmin Mukhida, Toby Roycroft and Ranga Silva. Also Gabriella Casemore,
Zul Mukhida, Ruth Raudsepp, Philippa Smith and Gus Ferguson.

For the use of their library photographs, grateful thanks are due to: Chapel Studios p21 (John Heinrich),
p28 (Tim Garrod); Eye Ubiquitous p4 (D Cumming), p14 (J Waterlow), p18 (P Seheult), p22, p26
(L Fordyce); James Davis Travel Photography, p16;Topham Picturepoint p12, p24 (JT).
All other photographs belong to the Wayland Picture Library: p5 (top and bottom), p6; artwork on p8.

SCIENCE
MAGIC
WITH WATER

CHRIS OXLADE

GLOUCESTER PRESS
LONDON • NEW YORK • TORONTO • SYDNEY

Design
David West Children's Book
Design
Designer
Steve Woosnam Savage
Editor
Suzanne Melia
Illustrator
Ian Thompson
Model maker
Keith Newell

© Aladdin Books Ltd 1993
Created and designed by
N.W. Books
28 Percy Street
London W1P 9FF

First published in
Great Britain in 1993 by
Franklin Watts Ltd
96 Leonard Street
London EC2A 4RH

ISBN 0 7496 1092 1

A CIP catalogue record for this
book is available from the British
Library

CONTENTS

WATER MAGIC!

Water is the most common substance on Earth. You probably use water every day without realising what strange and magical properties it holds. Water can store energy, travel uphill and fill the gaps in other materials. It can even support some objects on a thin, stretchy skin that covers its surface. Water can travel around corners and cause other substances to magically disappear on contact. It is the natural star of your magic show.

BE AN EXPERT MAGICIAN

PREPARING YOUR ROUTINE

There is much more to being a magician than just doing tricks. It is important that you and your assistant practise your whole routine lots of times, so that your performance goes smoothly when you do it for real. You will be a more entertaining magician if you do.

PROPS

Props are all the bits and pieces of equipment that a magician uses during an act. This includes your clothes as well as the tricks themselves. It's a good idea to make a magician's trunk from a large box to keep all your props in. During your routine, you can dip into the trunk, pulling out all sorts of equipment and crazy objects (see Distraction). You could tell jokes about these objects.

PROPS LIST

Magic wand	Food colouring
Top hat	Paper
Waistcoat	Wax candle
Silk scarves	Plastic jug
Balloons	Cardboard
Paint	Eggs
Boxes	Straws
Plastic tubes	Ping-pong balls
Containers	Coat-hangers

Tissue paper	
Cotton wool	
Sticky-tape	

WHICH TRICKS?

Work out which tricks you want to put in your routine. Put in some long tricks and some short tricks. This will keep your audience interested. If you can, include a trick that you can keep going back to during the routine. Magicians call this a "running gag".

MAGICIAN'S PATTER

Patter is what you say during your routine. Good patter makes a routine much more interesting and allows it to run much more smoothly. It is a good way to entertain your audience during

the slower times in your routine. Try to make up a story for each trick. Remember to introduce yourself and your assistant at the start and to thank the audience at the end. Practise your patter when you practise your tricks.

DISTRACTION

Distraction is an important part of a magician's routine. By waving a colourful scarf in the air and telling a joke, you can take the audience's attention away from something you'd rather they didn't see!

KEEP IT SECRET

The best magicians never give away their secrets. If anyone asks how your tricks work, just reply "By magic!" Then you can impress people with your tricks

INTRODUCING MAGIC MANDY
AND THE
MEMORY BALL

Magic Mandy waves her wand to give the Memory Ball the power to remember!

Ask for a volunteer from the audience. Demonstrate how to spin the Memory Ball (using a finger and thumb). Ask your volunteer to spin the ball, let it spin for a few seconds, and then stop it (and keep holding it). Now touch the ball lightly with your wand and say "Remember Memory Ball!". When your volunteer lets go, the ball begins to spin again — the right way every time.

WHAT YOU NEED
Ping-pong ball
Cotton
Thick card or wood
Wire coat-hanger
Sticky tape

THE SCIENCE
BEHIND THE TRICK

When the ball is spun round, the inside surface pulls the water round too. So the water gradually begins to spin. When the ball is stopped, the water inside keeps spinning for a few seconds. If you let go before it stops, the water makes the ball spin again. The water keeps spinning because it has inertia. Inertia is what makes things difficult to start or to stop. Heavy things, such as cars, have lots of inertia.

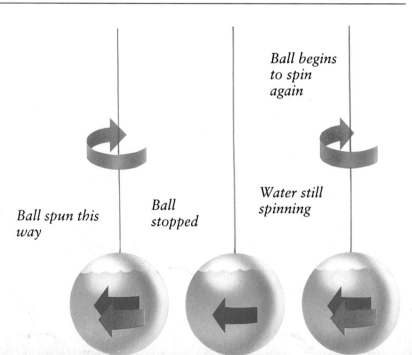

Ball spun this way

Ball stopped

Ball begins to spin again

Water still spinning

8

1 Make a base from thick card or wood. It should be about 40 cm by 20 cm. Bend a wire coat-hanger into an L shape.

2 Fix the wire to the base so that it stands firmly. Using a craft knife, cut a small hole in the ping-pong ball. Fill the ball with water.

3 Dry round the hole and seal it with sticky tape. Attach a long piece of thread near the hole with tape. Tie the other end of the thread to the end of the wire.

INTRODUCING MAGIC MARTIN
AND THE
RED ROSE GROWS TRICK

Magician or gardener? Green-fingered Magic Mike grows a red rose during his performance.

This trick takes a little while to work, so begin it at the start of your show and let it work while you perform your other tricks. Pour some plain water into the vase. Wave your wand and command the rose to grow! Put the vase to one side where your audience can see it. By the end of your show the rose will magically have turned red.

WHAT YOU NEED
Plastic tube
Thin card
Tissue paper
Cotton wool
Glass or vase
Sticky tape

THE SCIENCE
BEHIND THE TRICK

The water gradually soaks into the cotton wool and then up into the tissue paper flower. The food colouring mixes with the water and is carried into the tissue paper. So the flower turns red. The water flows into the flower because of capillary action. This is where water is drawn up into tiny spaces. There are thousands of tiny spaces between the fibres of the cotton wool and tissue paper. In real plants, water also moves up the stem to the leaves because of capillary action.

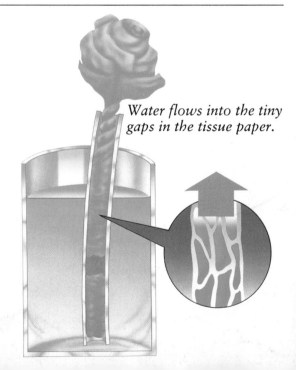

Water flows into the tiny gaps in the tissue paper.

10

GETTING PREPARED

1 Make leaves from card and attach them

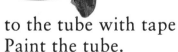

to the tube with tape Paint the tube.

2 Scrunch up a piece of tissue into a rose shape and twist the corners together. Push the twist into the top of the tube.

3 Put two drops of food colouring into the other end of the tube and fill the rest of the tube with cotton wool.

4 Put the prepared flower into an empty glass or vase. Fill a jug with water ready to pour into the glass.

11

INTRODUCING MAGIC MARIA
AND THE
BEWILDERING BOTTLE TRICK

The audience gasp as Magic Mandy turns red into yellow with this strange bottle.

Put the Bewildering Bottle onto your table. Place a glass under the tube to catch the water. Announce that you will now change red into yellow. Carefully pour red liquid into the floating container. Yellow water will begin to pour out of the tube. Your audience will think that the bottle is magically changing the colour of the water.

WHAT YOU NEED
Large plastic drinks bottle
Plastic tube
Sticky putty or sealant
Plastic glass
Coloured paper

THE SCIENCE BEHIND THE TRICK

As water is poured into the inner container, it gets heavier. As the inner container gets heavier, it sinks further down into the yellow water, pushing it out of the way. The level of the yellow water rises until it flows out of the tube. The amount of yellow water that is pushed out of the way is the same as the amount of water that is poured into the floating container. This is called displacement

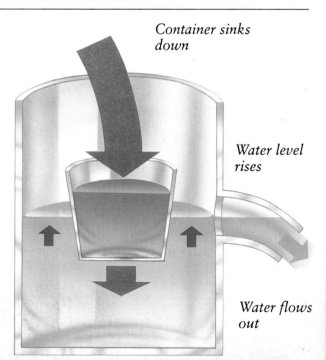

Container sinks down

Water level rises

Water flows out

1 Using a craft knife, carefully cut off the top of the bottle and paint it. When it is dry, cover it in a sheet of coloured paper with star shapes cut out of it.

2 Cut a hole in the side of the bottle and push in a piece of plastic tube. Seal around the hole with sticky putty or sealant. Paint the tube. Fill the bottle with yellow water and put the plastic container inside.

INTRODUCING MAGIC MALCOLM
AND THE
FAITHFUL FOUNTAIN

Magic Malcolm defies gravity to make water flow uphill and produce a fountain.

Before you start, put a dish underneath to catch the water. To start the fountain, secretly squeeze the bulldog clip to let the water flow. Say some magic words at the same time, and tap the fountain with your magic wand. To stop the fountain, secretly let the clip close again.

THE SCIENCE BEHIND THE TRICK

When the bulldog clip is released, water pours down the straw from the bottle. The air in the bottle spreads out to fill the space. This means the pressure in the bottle goes down. The pressure in the air outside the bottle is greater. It pushes down on the water in the plastic glass and makes the water go up the straw to make the fountain. It works a bit like a vacuum cleaner. The bottle "sucks" water up to make the fountain. When you close the clip, the water stops flowing out of the bottle. The fountain stops because the pressure stops going down.

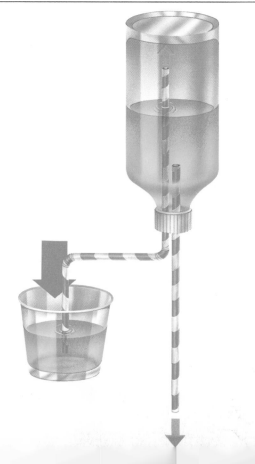

1 Drill two holes in the bottle top. Put straws through the holes and bend them as shown. Glue around the holes with sealant.

2 Stick together two cardboard boxes to make the stand. Make two small holes in the bottom box and feed through the longer straw.

3 Put some water in the bottle. Clip the bulldog clip on the bottom straw. Attach the bottle with the stand upside down.

INTRODUCING MAGIC MANDY
AND THE
INVISIBLE DRAWING

The pictures are invisible, but Magic Mandy can see each as clear as day.

Ask the audience to call out their favourite animals. Draw the first animal with the magic pen. Then keep drawing the first animal, no matter what is called out. For example, if the first animal called was a dog, draw a dog every time. Put the finished drawings into the box and ask a volunteer to choose one. Say that you think the chosen picture is a dog. Paint over the picture. The dog will appear!

WHAT YOU NEED
Candle
Card
White paper
Cardboard box
Water-based paint
Paint brush

THE SCIENCE
BEHIND THE TRICK

Candle wax is made from oil. Oily things do not mix well with water. That's why wax is used to protect surfaces from water. The wax lines on the picture are invisible until the water-based paint is added. Where there is no wax, the paint soaks into the paper, making it green. The water runs off the wax, leaving white lines.

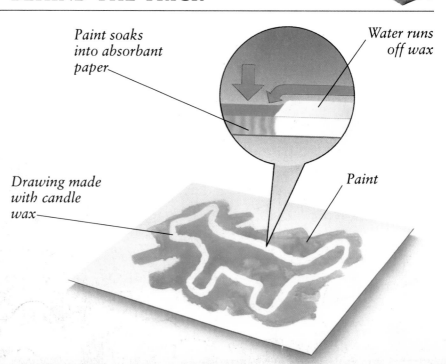

Paint soaks into absorbant paper

Water runs off wax

Drawing made with candle wax

Paint

16

1 Sharpen the candle using a craft knife. Cover it with card and add moons and stars. This will be your magic pen.

2 Decorate the box with magic symbols. Mix some water-based paint in a jar. Cut some sheets of paper to draw on.

INTRODUCING MAGIC MALCOLM
AND THE
BOTTLE THAT NEVER EMPTIES

Empty or full? Magic Malcolm baffles the audience with this strange, magical bottle.

WHAT YOU NEED
Large plastic drinks bottle
Plastic tube (about 1.5 cm wide)
Sticky putty or sealant

This trick makes a good "running gag" for your performance. Keep a finger over the hole and tip the bottle up. Water will pour out. Now turn the bottle upright and tip it up again. This proves that it's "empty". Put the bottle and glass to one side and perform another trick. Later, repeat the same sequence. Amazingly, there will be more water in the bottle!

THE SCIENCE BEHIND THE TRICK

When you take your finger off the hole, water flows up the tube. The water level in the bottle goes down a bit. The water in the tube pours out when you tip up the bottle. With the hole blocked, water cannot flow up the tube. This is because air cannot get into the space above the water.

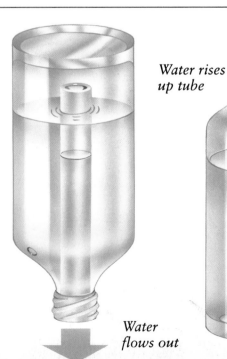

Water flows out

Hole unblocked

Water rises up tube

18

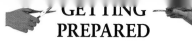
1 Cut a piece of plastic tube to about 1 cm less than the height of the bottle.

2 Push the tube into the bottle. Use a piece of folded card to wedge the tube in. Make sure that no water can escape. Glue the tube into place with sealant. Paint and decorate the bottle.

3 Cut a tiny hole near the neck of the bottle. Fill the bottle with coloured water using a funnel.

19

INTRODUCING MAGIC MIKE
AND THE
GLASS THAT NEVER FILLS

Magic Mike has the unfillable glass under his spell. As soon as it's full, it's empty again!

Pour water into the glass until it's half full. The glass will not empty yet. Now slowly fill it to the brim. Quickly tap the glass with your wand and command it to empty. The water will magically drain away!

WHAT YOU NEED
Cardboard boxes
Plastic glass
Small bowl
Bendy straws
Sticky putty or sealant

THE SCIENCE
BEHIND THE TRICK

The water drains away because the straws make a siphon. When the water in the glass is deep enough, the tube fills with water and the siphon begins to work. It keeps going until the glass is empty.

Glass half full

Glass full

Siphon tube not full

Tube fills

Siphon action starts

GETTING PREPARED

1 Using two cardboard boxes, make a stand as shown. Paint it and decorate it with cut out stars.

2 Cut a small hole in the bottom of the plastic container. Make a tube from bendy straws and seal one end into the container.

3 Make three small holes in the lower box and feed the straws through as shown.

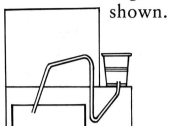

INTRODUCING MAGIC MIKE
AND THE
ROUND THE BEND TRICK

Magic Mike sends the audience round the bend! Is the water red or yellow?

Hold the board upright in front of you, gripping it as shown in the picture. Now announce that you can change red water into yellow, simply by tilting the tubes. Tilt one way and then the other. The level will stay the same in both tubes and it will look as though the red water changes to yellow as it passes under your hands.

WHAT YOU NEED
Plastic tube
Thick card

THE SCIENCE BEHIND THE TRICK

When the tubes are held upright, the water level is the same on each side. This is because water always finds its own level. When you tilt the tubes, the water moves around so that the levels remain the same on both sides. The depth is the same when measured from the lowest part of the tube, even though there is now more water on one side of the tube than the other.

Lowest part of tube

Water at same depth

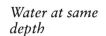

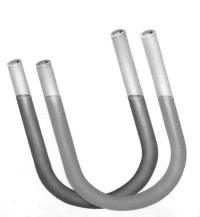

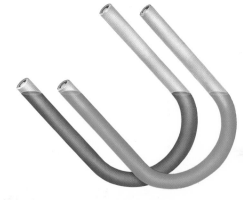

22

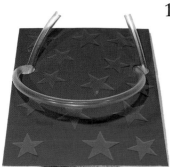

1 Cut a piece of card about 50 cm by 30 cm. Cut two pieces of tube about 100 cm long. Make two holes in the card and feed the tubes through. Fill the tubes to the same level with coloured water, and cover the holes with card.

INTRODUCING MAGIC MIKE
AND THE
SHOOTING STARS

With a flourish of his magic wand, Magic Mike sends the stars shooting through the water.

WHAT YOU NEED
Sweet wrappers
Wooden dowel
Glass bowl
Washing-up liquid

Wave your magic wand in front of your audience and tell them a story about its magical powers. "Legend says that this magic wand once belonged to the wizard Merlin" might be a good start. Ask a volunteer to watch the stars. As you do, secretly dip the end of the wand into the washing-up liquid. Tap the centre of the water with the wand. The stars will shoot to the edge of the bowl.

THE SCIENCE
BEHIND THE TRICK

Water is made up of millions of tiny particles called molecules which all cling to each other. This makes the surface of water like a stretchy skin. The skin can support light, flat objects like the paper stars. Detergents, such as washing-up liquid, break down surface tension. When the washing-up liquid touches the water, the skin breaks in the middle. Surface tension pulls the stars to the edge of the bowl as the skin itself breaks apart.

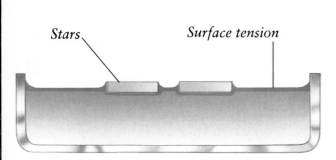

Stars   *Surface tension*

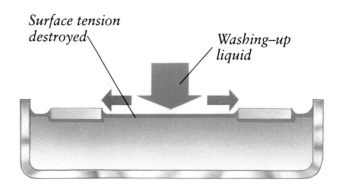

Surface tension destroyed   *Washing–up liquid*

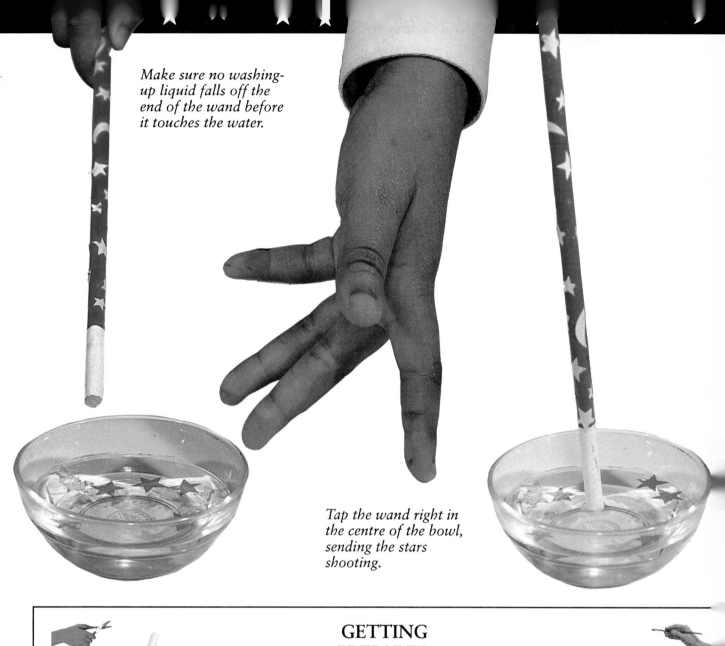

Make sure no washing-up liquid falls off the end of the wand before it touches the water.

Tap the wand right in the centre of the bowl, sending the stars shooting.

GETTING PREPARED

1 Make your magic wand. Cut a piece of dowelling about 30 cm long. Paint the middle red and about 4 cm at each end white. Decorate it with magic symbols.

2 Cut some stars from coloured sweet wrappers. Carefully float them in a bowl of water. Put some washing-up liquid in a glass.

INTRODUCING MAGIC MARIA
AND THE
SINK OR SWIM TRICK

Magic Maria stuns the audience with an egg raising trick!

Start with the turntable turned so that the glass containing the unsalted water is at the front. Announce that you will now make the egg float. Cover the box with the cloth. Wave your wand over the cloth while you secretly turn the turntable. Remove the cloth to reveal a magically floating egg!

THE SCIENCE BEHIND THE TRICK

Whether an object floats or sinks depends on its density. Density measures how much an object weighs compared to its size. An egg is slightly denser than plain water. This means that it just sinks to the bottom of a glass. When salt is added to water, it gets more dense. When enough is added, the water becomes more dense than the egg. Now the egg floats instead of sinking.

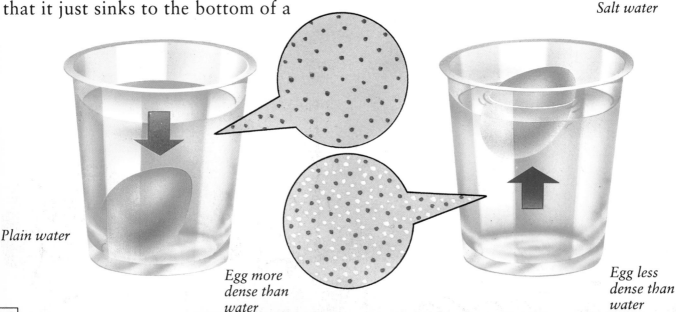

Salt water

Plain water

Egg more dense than water

Egg less dense than water

26

1 Cut the top and bottom off the box and decorate it with stars.

2 Fill one glass with plain water and one with salt water.

3 Make a turntable to fit inside the box. Decorate the front and back the same way.

HINTS AND TIPS

Here are some hints and tips for making your props. Good props will make your act look more professional. So spend time making and decorating your props, and look after them carefully. As well as the special props you need for each trick, try to make some general props such as a waistcoat and magic wand.

Decorate your props with magic shapes cut from coloured paper. Paint bottles and tubes with oil-based paint.

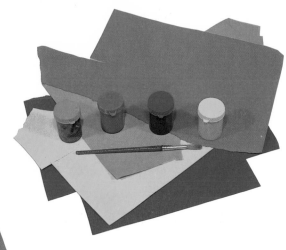

Make coloured water by adding food colouring to tap water. You only need a few drops of colour in a jug of water.

You will need sticky-tape and glue to make props. Double-sided tape might also be useful. You can use sticky putty or special plastic sealant to make water-proof joints.

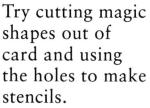

Try cutting magic shapes out of card and using the holes to make stencils.

Your act will look extra professional if you make a proper stage set. This is easy if you have a backcloth to hang behind the stage. A large piece of black cloth would be most effective. Use silver paint to create stars and moons. Decorate pieces of cloth to throw over your table. The overall effect should be a set that creates an atmosphere of mystery and magic.

Make your own magician's clothes. Try to find an old hat and waistcoat to decorate. If you can find some silvery material, cut our stars and moons and sew them on. An alternative is sequins. Use anything that is shiney and dramatic so you look professional.

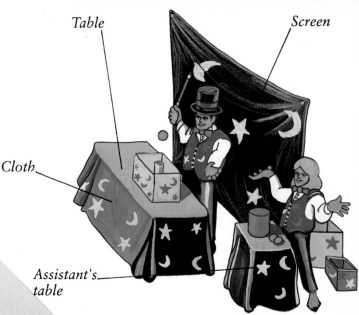

Table

Screen

Cloth

Assistant's table

Make a magician's table by draping a cloth over a table. You can put the props underneath out of sight.

GLOSSARY

CAPILLARY ACTION The rising or falling of water in contact with a solid.

DENSITY The heaviness of a substance of a particular volume.

DISPLACEMENT The amount of water pushed aside by an object when it is immersed or floating.

INERTIA The resistance of an object to any change of direction or movement.

MOLECULES The smallest naturally occurring particles of a substance.

PRESSURE The squeezing or pressing when force is applied to a substance and there is no room for it to change shape.

SIPHON ACTION The force which causes a liquid to flow through a narrow tube because of differences in pressure.

SURFACE TENSION the molecular force of a liquid that pulls it into the smallest possible area, making water drops and forming a curved surface (meniscus) on a glass of water.

VACUUM A space which contains no matter.